N
W
E
S
QLD
QUEENSLAND
SA
SOUTH
AUSTRALIA
NSW
NEW SOUTH WALES
ACT
AUSTRALIAN
CAPITAL
TERRITORY
VIC
VICTORIA
TAS
TASMANIA
AF584862

KYLE SURRY

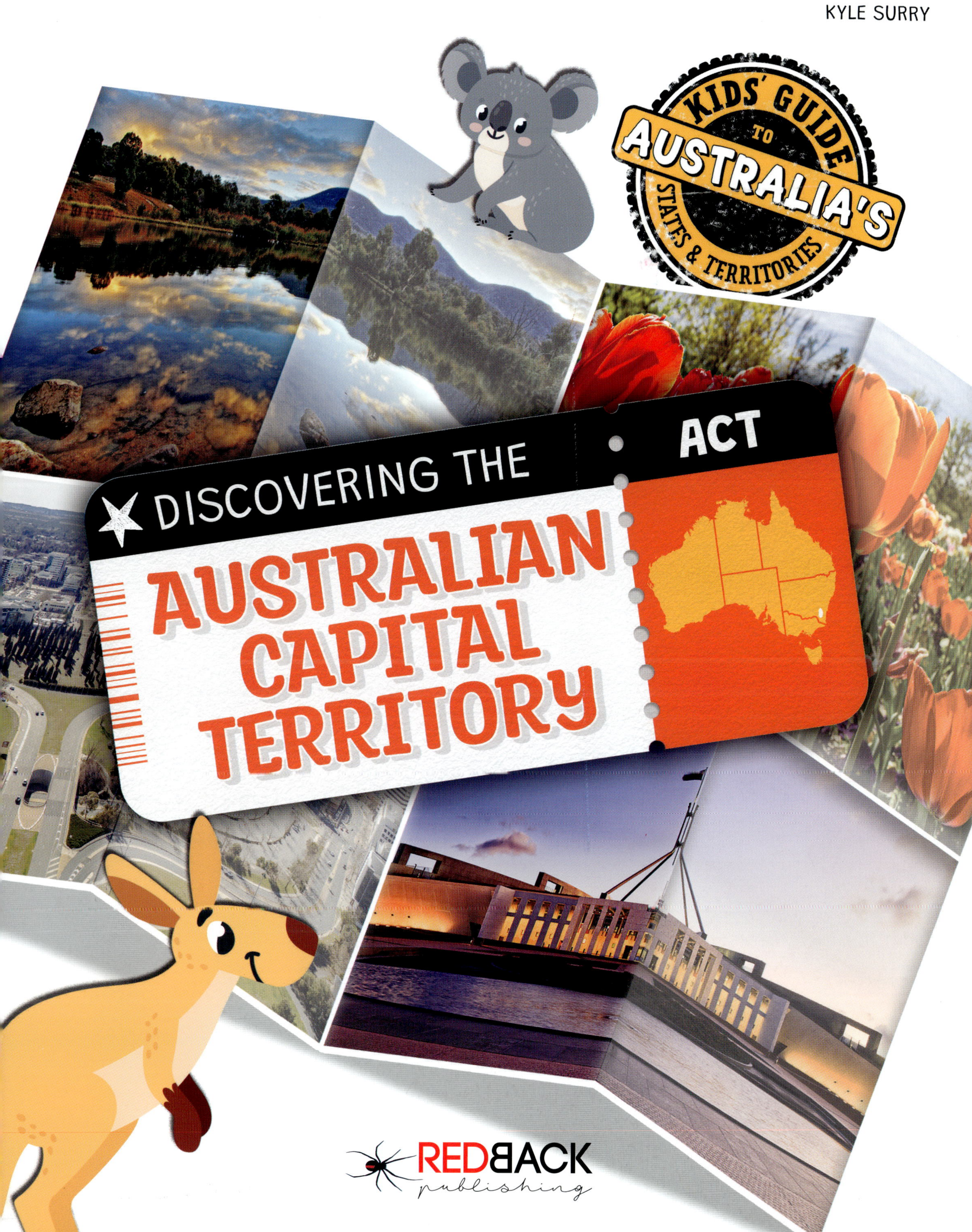

DISCOVERING THE AUSTRALIAN CAPITAL TERRITORY

REDBACK publishing

First Published 2026 by
Redback Publishing
Suite 6, 13a Narabang Way,
Belrose NSW 2085
Australia

www.redbackpublishing.com
orders@redbackpublishing.com

ISBN 978-1-761400-60-5

Author: Kyle Surry
Editors: Lucinda Dodds and Emma Dobinson
Designer: Redback Publishing

Original illustrations © Redback Publishing 2026
Originated by Redback Publishing

Acknowledgements
Abbreviations: l—left, r—right, b—bottom, t—top, c—centre, m—middle
We would like to thank the following for permission to reproduce photographs: (Images © shutterstock, Alamy) p4-5 - Steve Tritton / Shutterstock.com, p5br - droneconcept2023 / Shutterstock.com, p10 - By Unknown author - Unknown source, Public Domain, https://commons.wikimedia.org/w/index.php?curid=389501, p13ml - Stanley Goodhew (via Miles Goodhew) - Gwen Jack Leslie Bagnall Rupert BimberiUploaded by berichard, CC BY-SA 2.0, https://commons.wikimedia.org/w/index.php?curid=12643194, p17tr - Christopher Lee- Up Up Up Aerial Imaging - Own work, CC BY-SA 4.0, https://commons.wikimedia.org/w/index.php?curid=44701555, p17bl - Grahamec - Own work, CC BY-SA 4.0, https://commons.wikimedia.org/w/index.php?curid=64629807, p22-23 - Ragil HTP / Shutterstock.com, p23mr - Alexandre.ROSA / Shutterstock.com, p25mr - Squiresy92 including elements modified from Sodacan - Own work, Public Domain, https://commons.wikimedia.org/w/index.php?curid=43893649, p29tr - Martyman at the English Wikipedia, CC BY-SA 3.0, https://commons.wikimedia.org/w/index.php?curid=473784, p30 - EQRoy / Shutterstock.com

A catalogue record for this book is available from the National Library of Australia

CONTENTS

A Long Time Ago 4
Settlers and Colonisers 6
Where Is the ACT? 8
Canberra 10
Landscapes in the ACT 12
Bimberi Peak 13
How Many People? 14
Cities and Towns 16
Transport in the ACT 18
Tourism 20
Government of the ACT 22
Flags of the ACT 24
Emblems of the ACT 25
Royal Australian Mint 26
Parliament House 27
Namadgi National Park 28
Learning in the ACT 30
Glossary 31
Index 32

Parliament House

A LONG TIME AGO

Who Was There First?

Canberra and the ACT are on the traditional lands of the Ngunnawal people. Their meeting grounds, called Kamberra, were near Black Mountain.

The local Bogong moth feast used to be an annual event that drew the Ngunnawal people to the area for meetings and trade.

Moth Ascending the Capital, a sculpture of Bogong moths

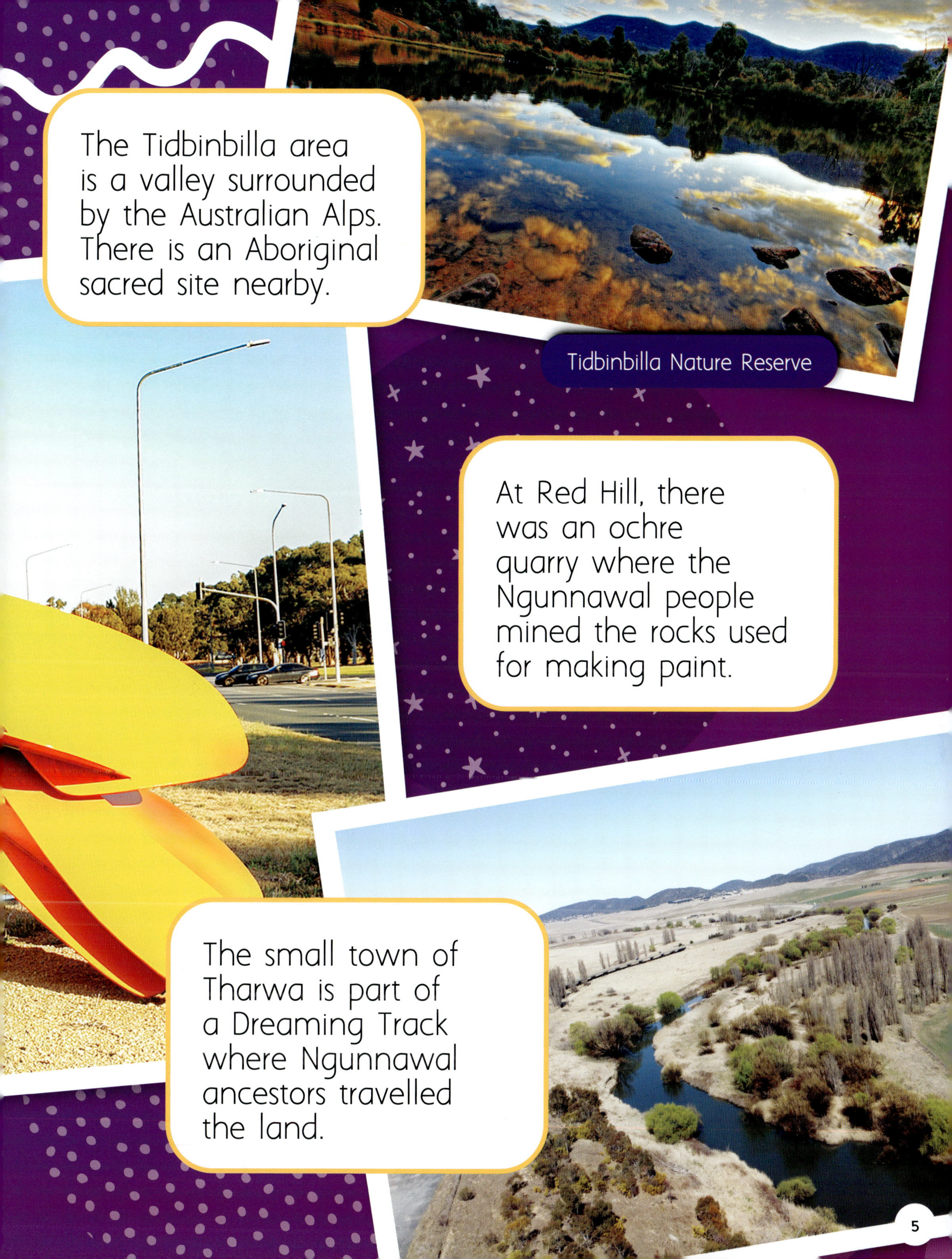

The Tidbinbilla area is a valley surrounded by the Australian Alps. There is an Aboriginal sacred site nearby.

Tidbinbilla Nature Reserve

At Red Hill, there was an ochre quarry where the Ngunnawal people mined the rocks used for making paint.

The small town of Tharwa is part of a Dreaming Track where Ngunnawal ancestors travelled the land.

SETTLERS AND COLONISERS

Early 1800s

When European settlers arrived in the ACT, they colonised areas that had been in traditional ownership for thousands of years. Sheep replaced the native animals on the land and forests were cleared for pastures.

1823 to 1830s

Large properties were established on the land now occupied by Canberra. They included Canberry, Springbank, Duntroon and Yarralumla.

1911

The State of NSW transferred the land for the ACT to the Commonwealth of Australia.

1913

At a large ceremony on 12 March, Canberra became the capital of Australia.

WHERE IS THE ACT?

Canberra is in the north of the Australian Capital Territory, and is completely surrounded by the state of New South Wales. Canberra is Australia's capital city.

The short way of writing this area's name is ACT. The area of the ACT is less than 1% of the total area of Australia.

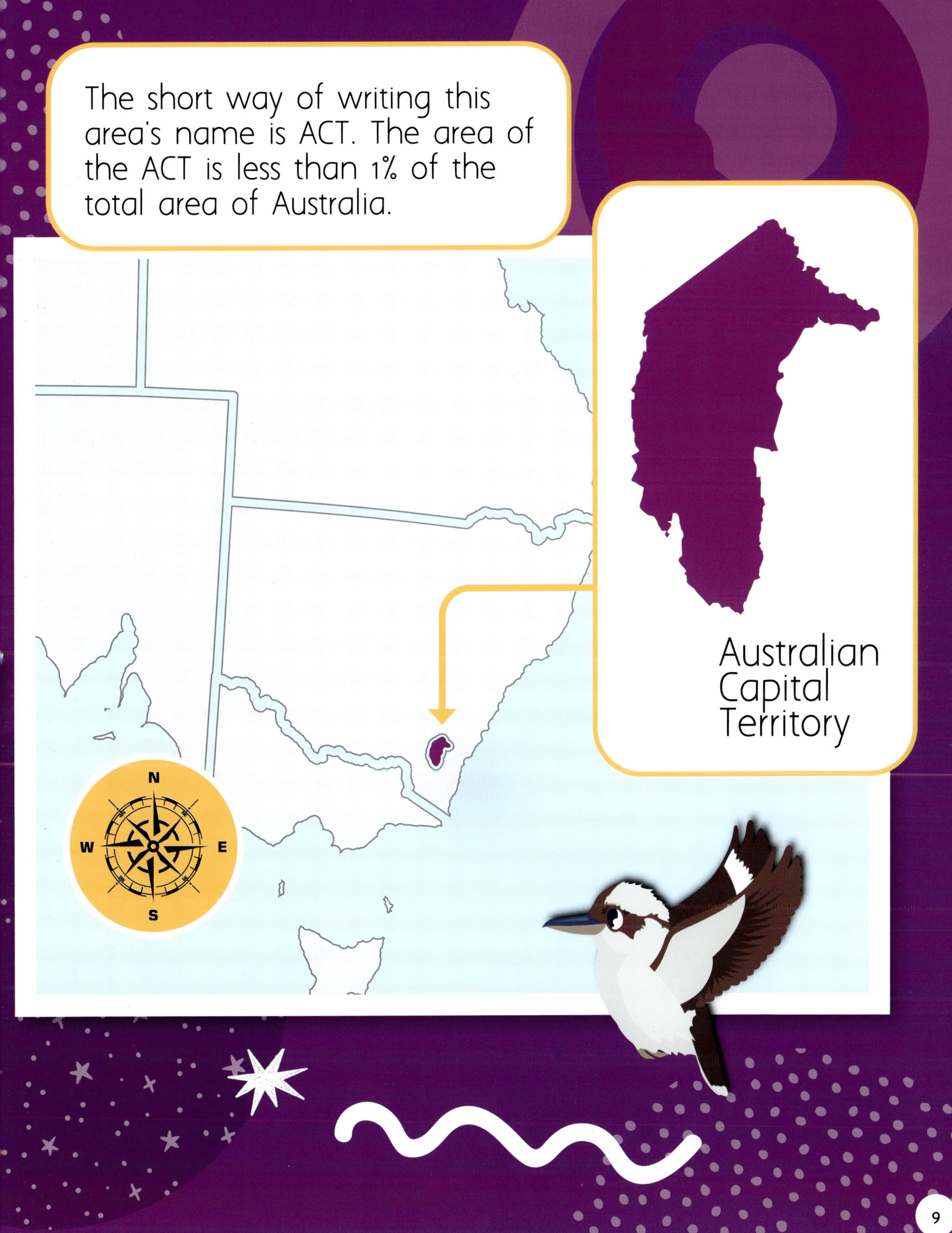

CANBERRA

Naming the Capital City

The name of the new capital city was kept a secret until the wife of the Governor General announced it at a ceremony in 1913. Taking a card from a golden box, she read the name Canberra to the waiting crowds.

The designer of the city of Canberra was Walter Burley Griffin, an American architect. He won a competition to design the new city in 1911. The layout of Canberra is geometric, with circular roads, long avenues and whole areas shaped like triangles and hexagons.

Lake Burley Griffin

This lake was a part of Griffin's design, but it was not created until 1963, after a dam was built on the Molonglo River to provide the water.

Civic

From the 1920s to the 1940s, Canberra's shopping and business centre developed based on two large buildings on Northbourne Avenue. The area became known as Civic.

LANDSCAPES IN THE ACT

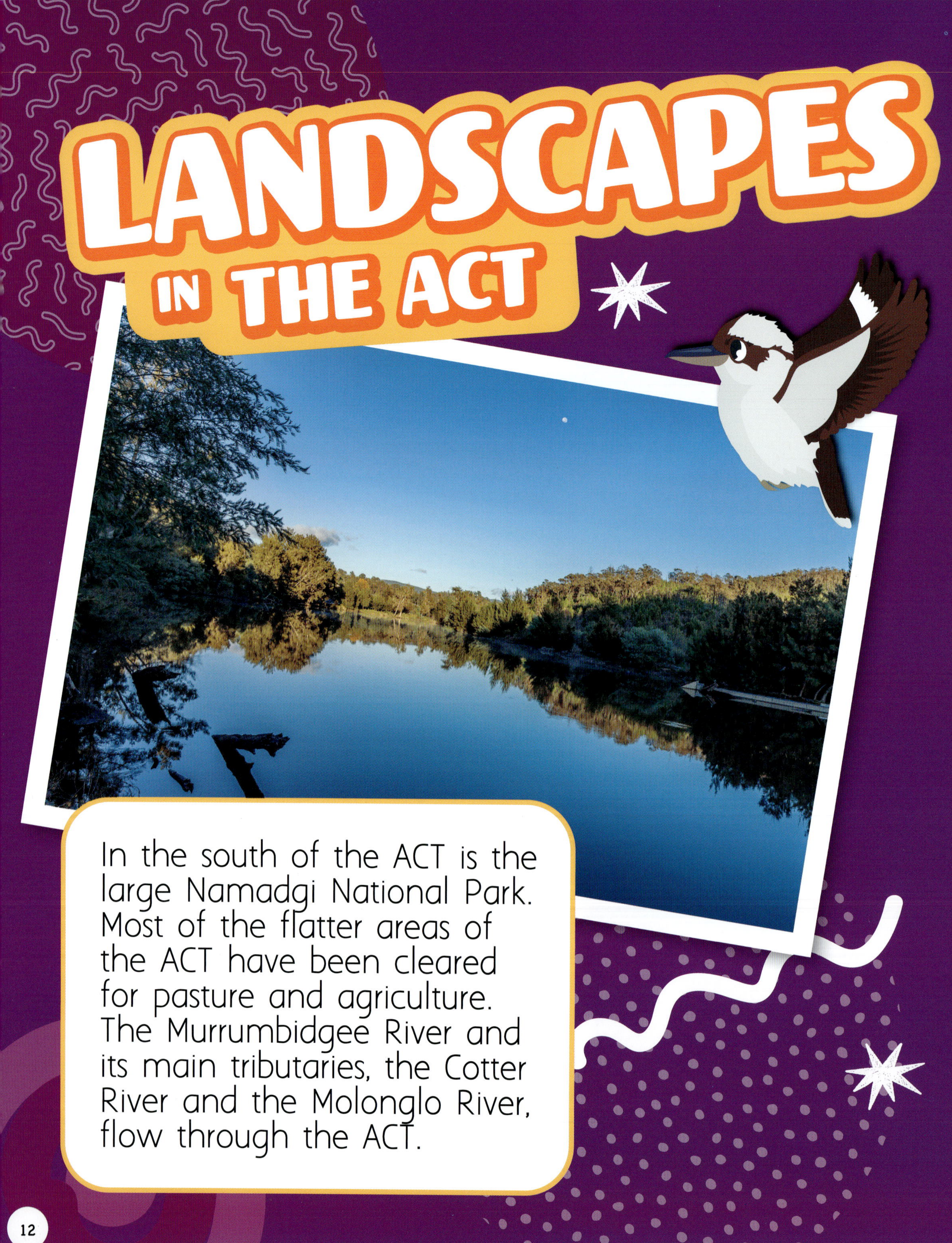

In the south of the ACT is the large Namadgi National Park. Most of the flatter areas of the ACT have been cleared for pasture and agriculture. The Murrumbidgee River and its main tributaries, the Cotter River and the Molonglo River, flow through the ACT.

BIMBERI PEAK

The highest mountain in the ACT is Bimberi Peak. It rises to 1,911 metres, which is only about 300 metres lower than Mount Kosciuszko, which is the highest mountain in Australia. Bimberi Peak is part of the Great Dividing Range, which runs along most of the east coast of Australia.

HOW MANY PEOPLE?

There are about 482,000 people living in the city of Canberra and its nearby areas.

(ABS 2024)

Most of the population of the ACT live in the city of Canberra. There is a small population of people living in other parts of the ACT.

The people in the ACT have a high level of education compared to the rest of Australia.

The main employer in the ACT is the Federal Government.

CITIES AND TOWNS

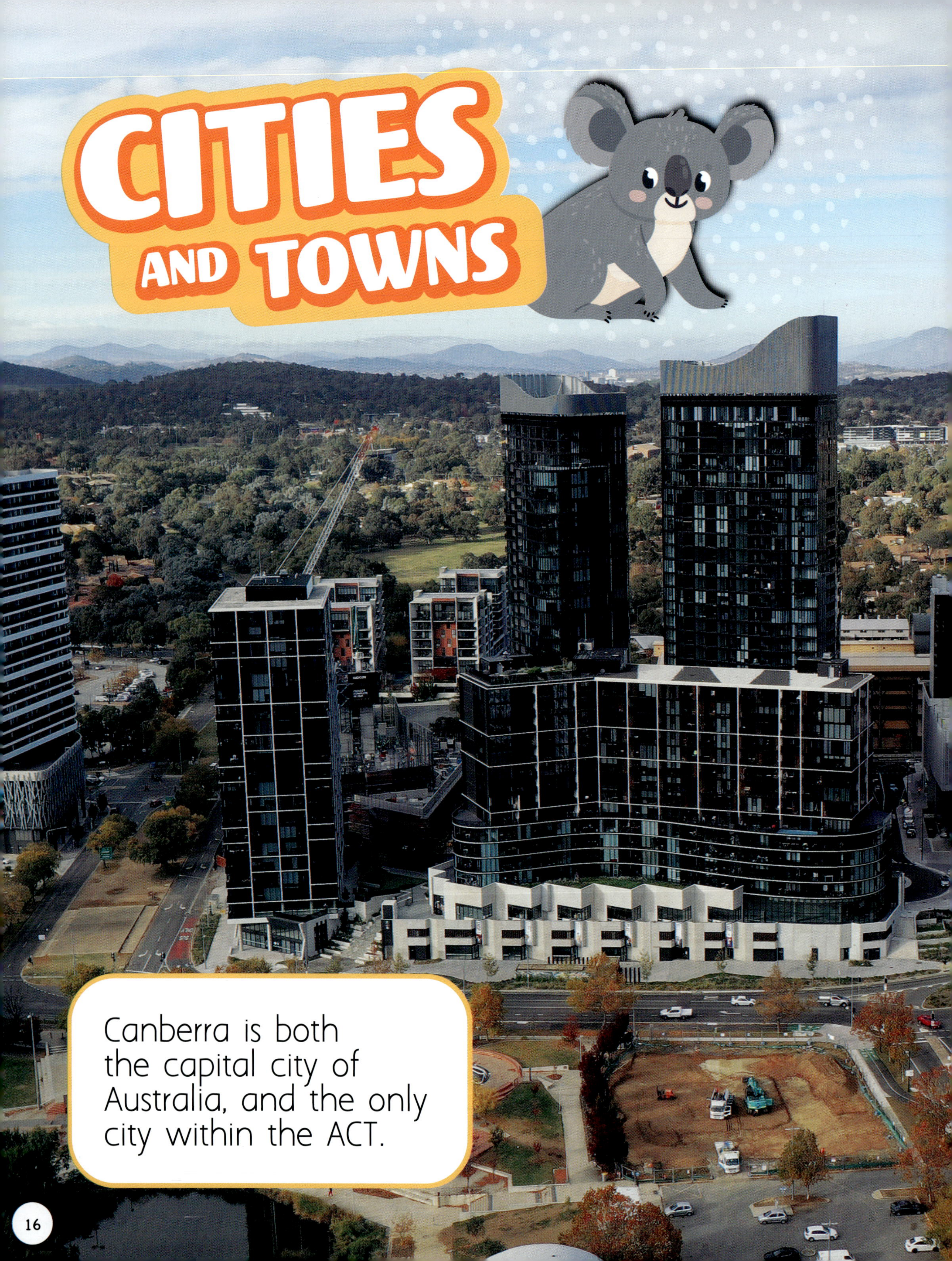

Canberra is both the capital city of Australia, and the only city within the ACT.

Beyond the city of Canberra and its suburbs, there are a number of small towns and villages in the ACT including:
Hall
Tharwa
Uriarra
Williamsdale

TRANSPORT IN THE ACT

Roads

Roads in the ACT were dirt tracks in the colonial era. Today, Canberra is known for its planned roads, roundabouts and long avenues.

Airport

Originally a sheep paddock, the busy Canberra Airport now has both international and domestic flights.

Railway

Although it is Australia's capital, Canberra does not have a railway service. The only train station in the ACT is in the suburb of Kingston.

Bridges

There are many bridges in the ACT, but the oldest surviving one is the Tharwa Bridge, over the Murrumbidgee River. It dates from 1895 and is still in use.

TOURISM

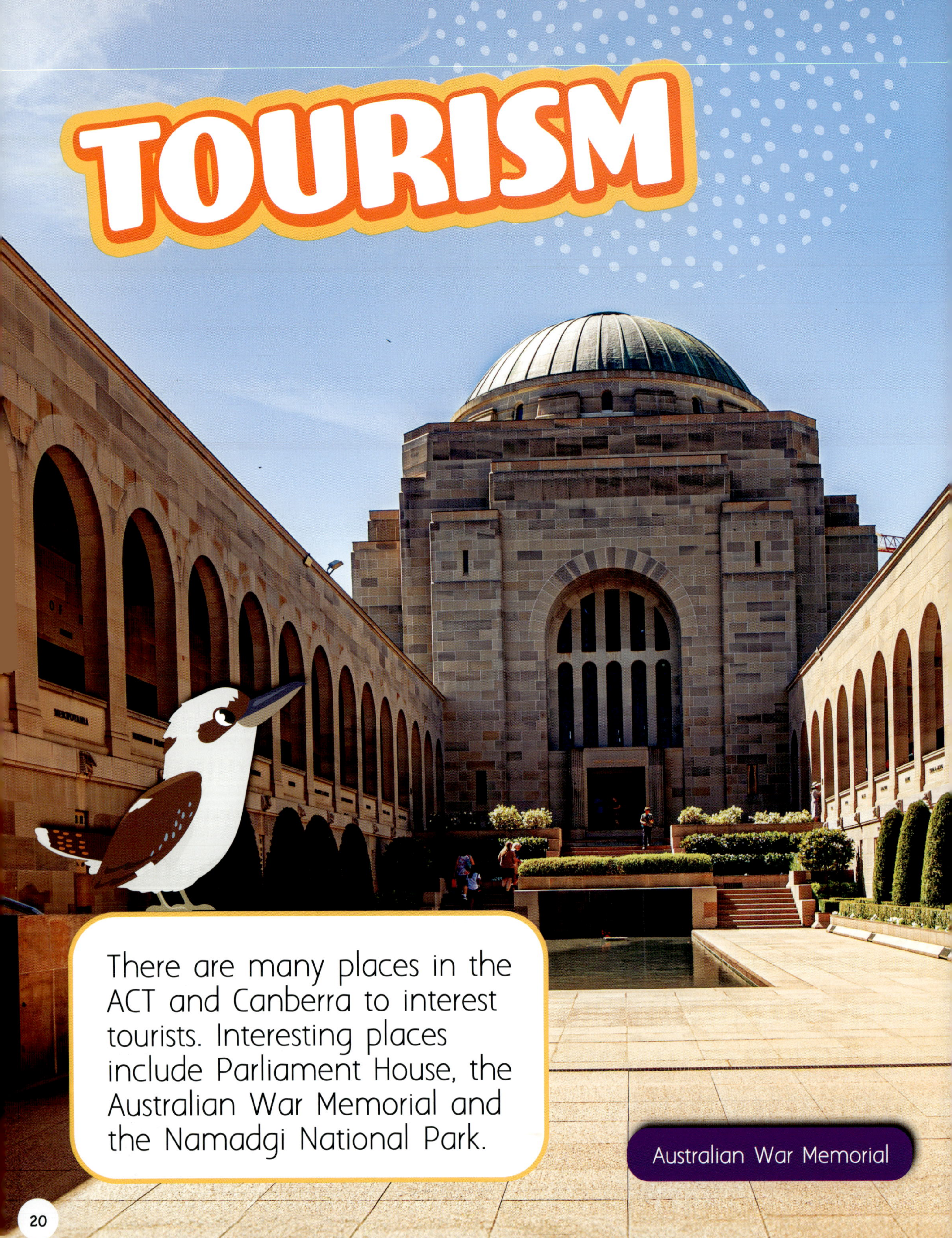

There are many places in the ACT and Canberra to interest tourists. Interesting places include Parliament House, the Australian War Memorial and the Namadgi National Park.

Australian War Memorial

Floriade

Floriade is an annual spring flower festival that attracts visitors from Australia and overseas.

A visit to Canberra helps children understand the way the Australian Parliament operates.

School Excursions

Every year, thousands of students from around Australia visit Canberra on school excursions.

All the main sites of government provide educational programs for students.

GOVERNMENT OF THE ACT

Legislative Assembly for the ACT

This has the role of both a state government and a local council for the ACT. There are no local councils in the ACT. The Legislative Assembly has only one house, or section, in its Parliament. There are 25 elected members in the Legislative Assembly. They represent the five local electorates in the ACT.

Federal Parliament

As well as having elected politicians in its own territorial government, the ACT also elects:

- Two senators to the Australian Senate
- Three members of the Australian House of Representatives

Parliament House

The leader of the ACT Legislative Assembly is called the Chief Minister.

FLAGS OF THE ACT

Australian Aboriginal Flag

The Aboriginal Flag was first flown in 1971. It was designed by elder Harold Thomas in 1970.

What the flag represents:

Yellow Disc	The Sun and yellow ochre
Red	The land
Black	The Aboriginal people of Australia

ACT Flag

The ACT flag shows the Southern Cross and a part of Canberra's Coat of Arms.

The colours of blue, gold and white refer to the colours of the City of Canberra.

EMBLEMS OF THE ACT

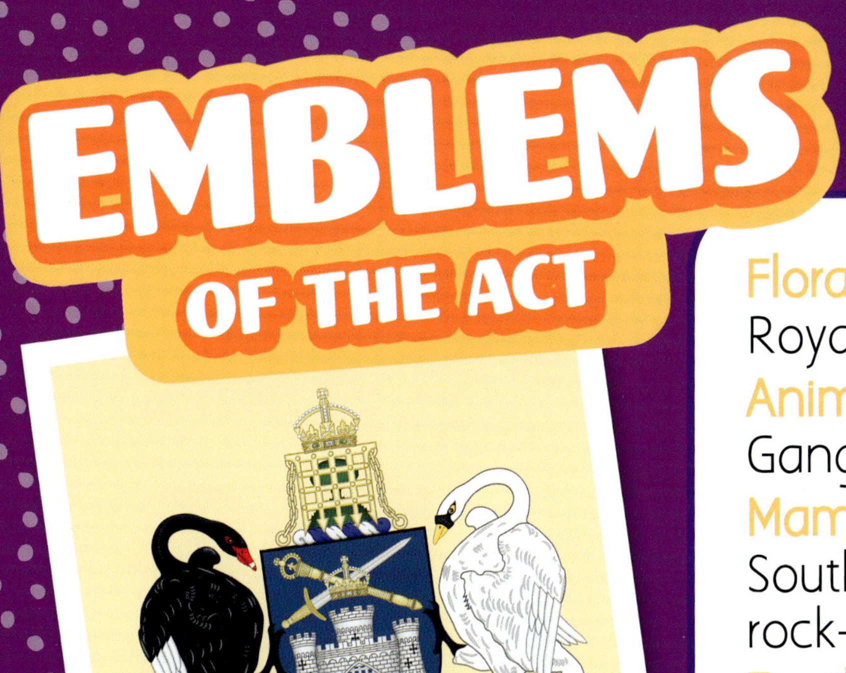

Floral Emblem
Royal bluebell

Animal Emblem
Gang-gang cockatoo

Mammal Emblem
Southern brush-tailed rock-wallaby

Fossil Emblem
Batocara mitchelli

The Coat of Arms

Each part of the Coat of Arms has a meaning:

Castle
A symbol of the city

Sword of Justice
A symbol for authority

Mace
A symbol of the power to make laws

Crown
A symbol of the Monarchy

Rose
The Rose of York is a symbol for government

Portcullis or Gate
Refers to the Westminster System of government

Gum tree
A symbol for growth

Swans
Symbols for the Aboriginal people and European settlers

Motto
Pro Rege, Lege et Grege which means 'For the Monarch, the Law and the People'

ROYAL AUSTRALIAN MINT

The Royal Australian Mint was opened in 1965, when it began making new coins for the changeover to decimal currency in 1966. The Royal Australian Mint has made coins for:

- Australia
- The Solomon Islands
- Vanuatu
- Tonga
- The Cook Islands
- Samoa

PARLIAMENT HOUSE

Parliament House in Canberra was opened in 1988. The building is designed to last for the next 200 years. The green colour of the Senate and the red colour of the House of Representatives are based on colours used by the British Parliament.

NAMADGI NATIONAL PARK

The Namadgi National Park covers over 40% of the ACT. In 2001, the Ngunnawal people were recognised as the park's traditional custodians.

There are about 400 Aboriginal sites of importance in the park, including the rock art at Yankee Hat.
Yankee Hat
Bushfires are a constant threat to the Namadgi National Park. They threaten forests, animals and sacred sites.

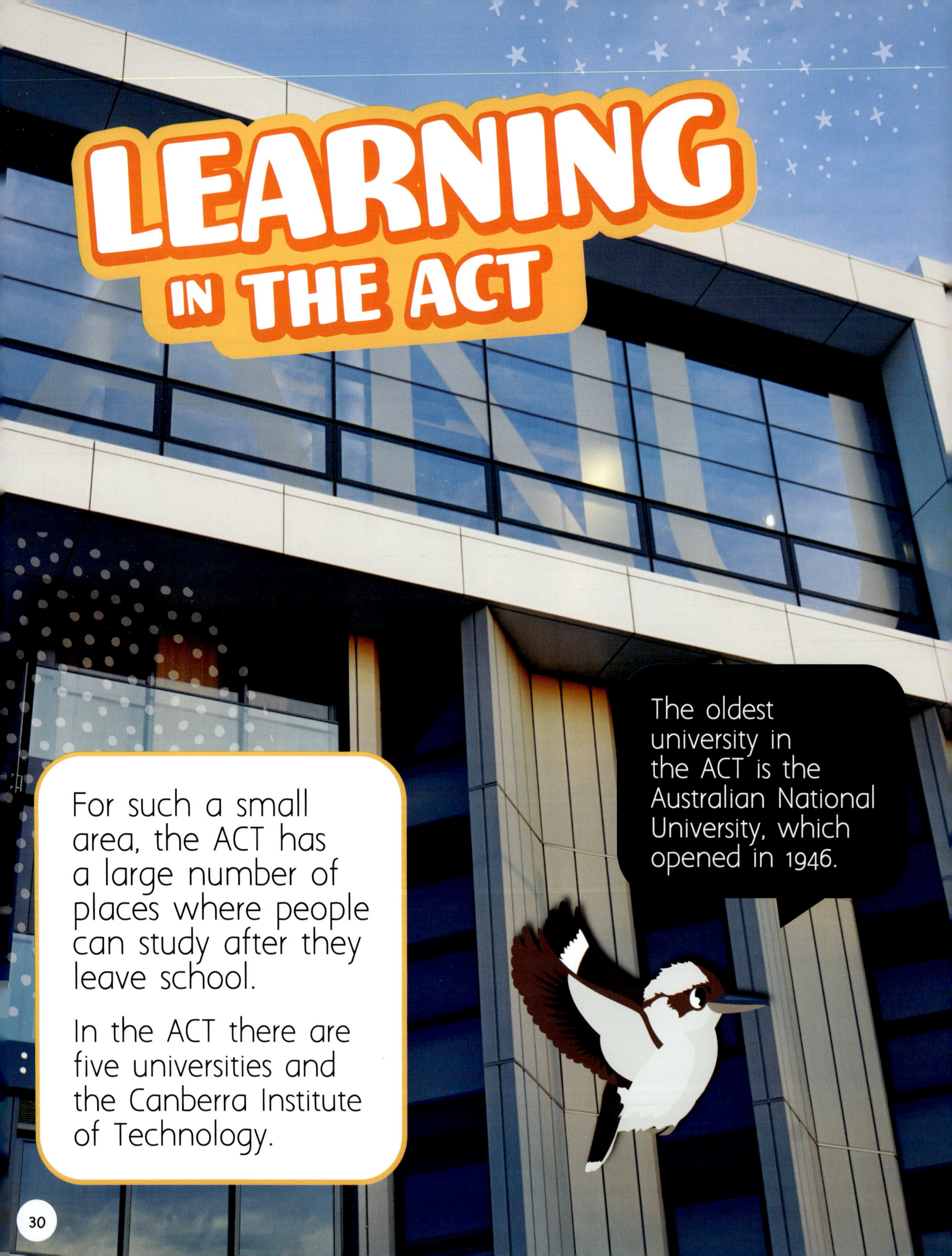

LEARNING IN THE ACT

For such a small area, the ACT has a large number of places where people can study after they leave school.

In the ACT there are five universities and the Canberra Institute of Technology.

The oldest university in the ACT is the Australian National University, which opened in 1946.

Glossary

architect person who designs buildings and towns

coat of arms design usually including a shield and symbols

colonial referring to the time between 1788 and Federation in 1901

custodians people who look after something

electorate area that an elected person represents

emblem symbol

grazed ate grass

House of Representatives part of the Australian Parliament

Monarchy government headed by a King or Queen

motto words that represent the values and ideals of a person or place

Senate part of the Australian Parliament

traditional something that is done as it was in the past

INDEX

bush fires 29
Civic 11
Floriade 21
Lake Burley Griffin 11
Legislative Assembly 22
Namadgi National Park 12, 20, 28, 29
Ngunnawal 4, 5, 28, 29
school excursions 21
Tharwa 5, 17, 19
Tidbinbilla 5
universities 30
Walter Burley Griffin 11

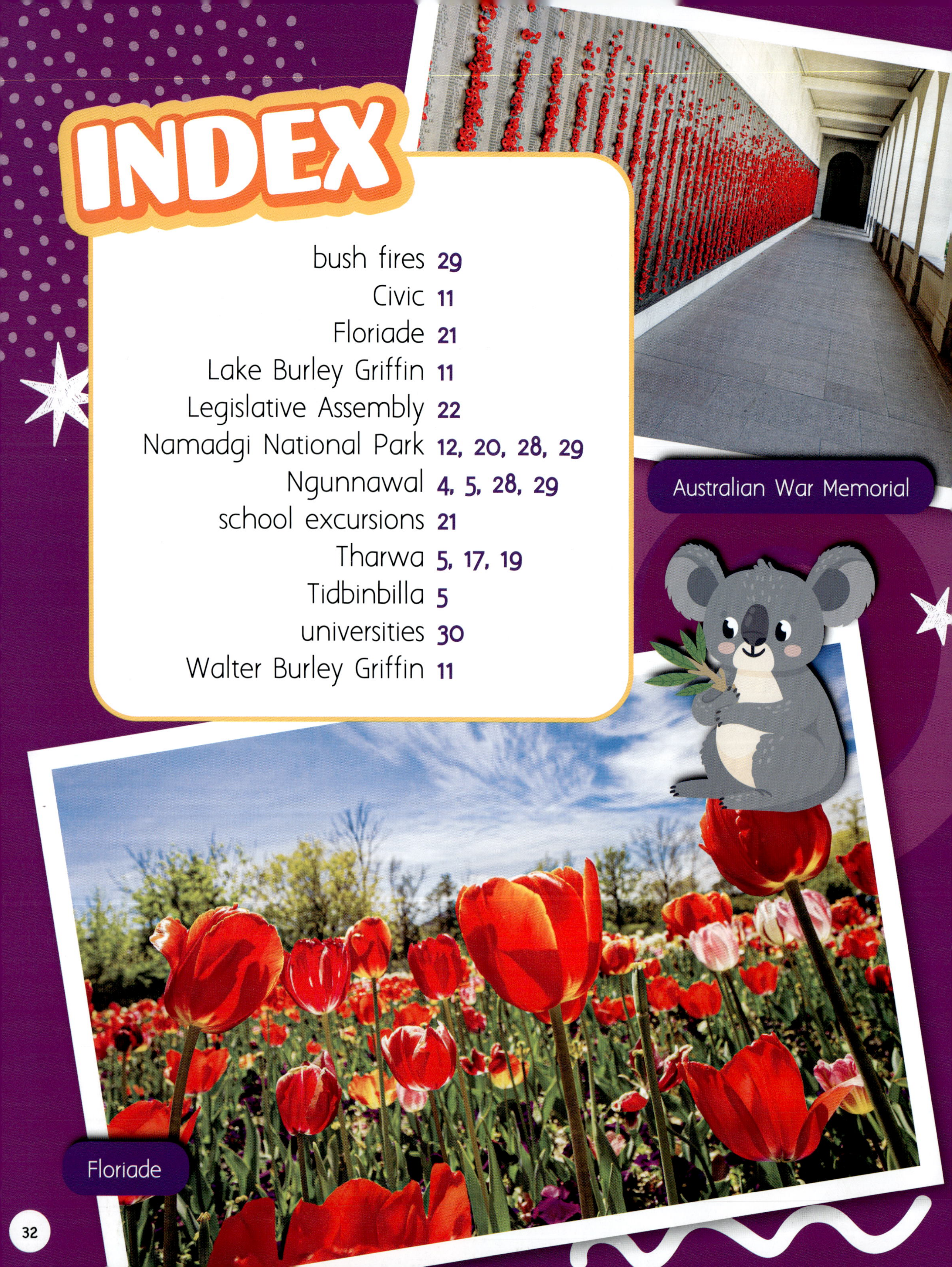

Australian War Memorial

Floriade

KIDS' GUIDE
TO
AUSTRALIA'S
STATES & TERRITORIES
WA
WESTERN
AUSTRALIA
NT
NORTHERN
TERRITORY